The Practical Guide to Revised Higher Literature

by

David Cockburn

© *D. Cockburn, 1991*
ISBN 0 7169 3168 0

ROBERT GIBSON · **Publisher**
17 Fitzroy Place, Glasgow, G3 7SF.

FOR THE CANDIDATE

This book is the companion to *The Practical Guide to Revised Higher English*. While the latter is a guide which concentrates on giving you practical advice about the examination, this book gives you advice about how to prepare and study the literature you have chosen for both the *Review of Personal Reading* and for *Paper II*. It is written with you in mind, and it will give you the confidence you need.

Other Books to Help You

Practical Guide to Revised Higher English
Practical Guide to Poetry
A Guide to Mass Media

CONTENTS

-1-

THE IMPORTANCE OF READING

There is no rush. It's Saturday. You sit down to breakfast. You notice a different packet of cereal. Instantly you make for it and voraciously digest the written text. Even if it's just the SELL-BY date and the E numbers. You can't help it. You're a reader.

But why do we read fiction — novels, short stories? One of the answers must be: 'for pleasure'. But there are other reasons, one of the most important of which is that, from the ideas that a book of fiction contains, we can learn something about ourselves, about others, and about the society in which the book is set. In other words about life.

There are two main reasons why we read (or watch plays or view films): to confirm our experience and to extend our experience. Often we enjoy a book because we identify with one of the main characters in it — he/she has the same background as ourselves, or is going through the same experiences, or is confronted with the same problems. In the middle of such a book we can find ourselves quite surprised by one of the character's reactions to a situation that we ourselves have recently experienced — to such an extent that we declare to ourselves: "But that's exactly how I felt last Tuesday . . .". The book, then, is confirming our experience, making us a bit more aware of how we feel, how we behave, how we are as people. Since all of us (quite naturally) are interested in self, we enjoy these books because they are saying something about self, even although what is said is coming through the made-up experiences of a character who exists only in the imagination.

I said that there were two reasons for reading. The other reason is that we enjoy having our experience extended: the novel occupies a world which we don't know but which we are keen to learn about, or it involves a character who is experiencing situations/problems/emotions which we have not undergone but by which we are fascinated and in which we are very interested. We may not know what it's like to be a brutish, over-bearing general who murders his king and then rules tyranically, yet we may read *Macbeth* to find out; in fact, we may well enjoy *Macbeth* precisely because we are not like that.

More than likely the two reasons come together in the same book, but nevertheless our enjoyment of a book can be ascribed to one or other or both of these reasons. Clearly, then, the books we read and enjoy (or don't read because we're bored by them) say quite a lot about ourselves. If we read a book because it confirms our experience, then that says something about the experiences we have undergone; it also says something about us that we enjoy reliving the experiences or reflecting on the experiences of others through the book we are reading. Clearly, too, if we lead dull, boring, trivial little lives, devoid of any imaginatively challenging stimuli, then we're going to be short of any experiences to bring to any given book.

Literature, then, poses a problem for young people: if the enjoyment of reading depends on the experiences of the reader, then how can young people, who just because they are young and therefore haven't accumulated much in the way of adult experience, how can these young people enjoy books? Much of what is presented in the way of literature to 17 year-olds really does require adult experience before it can be fully appreciated. This is not to patronise the young or to be superior to them — it is merely a fact of life. How can a 17 year-old identify with a 60 year-old salesman who is tired to the death? How can a 40 year-old for that matter understand what it's like to be an 80 year-old king who has given away his kingdom to ungrateful daughters? Yet clearly young people appreciate *Death of a Salesman* and the early middle-aged enjoy *King Lear*. So we bring more than just experience to literature: we need the ability to imagine the experiences of others and to understand how they think and feel. In so doing, we extend our imagination and develop our understanding: literature, then, can help us grow as human beings. Wisdom isn't just a quality to be found in literature: literature can be a means of developing wisdom in the reader.

I have spent some time stressing the importance of reading. You must not think of *Hamlet* or *To Kill a Mockingbird* or *Afternoons* as Fifth year texts suitable for Higher English, to be swallowed whole and regurgitated in the examination, but as experiences valuable in themselves and valuable in the contribution they can make to your development as a human being. What matters is your relationship with the texts you intend to study in your Higher English course — what they mean to you as an individual, what you get out of them. That means, of course, that you must be very familiar with the texts and that you have to spend a lot of time working out what they do mean to you. Once you have done that, then you can begin on the process of asking yourself how — the means by which — the author has brought about the reactions he has in you. The entire process is circular, however — as you get to know the text, the more you realise what it means to you, and the more you know what it means to you, the more you are aware of the techniques by which the author has brought about the reaction he has in you, and the more you are aware of the author's technique, the more you get to know the text. And so on.

This work obviously cannot be done the night before the examination; it has to be done as you study the text in class, using your time at home to read, re-read, reflect and respond. When it comes to studying any work of literature, film, television play, soap opera, whatever, bear in mind three questions which correspond to the stages outlined above:

(a) What is the novel/play/poem/film about?
(Getting to know the text.)

(b) What are the effects on me?
(How do I react — cry, laugh, feel sad, feel bored?)

(c) How have these effects been produced?
(What techniques has the author used to bring about this reaction in me?)

It has to be stressed, and it will be throughout this book, that skills in English aren't discrete — separate and compartmentalised. As we develop one skill, we affect the development of another. I've already referred to the circularity of the above process: our ability to answer *(a)* makes the answering of *(b)* easier, and our skills at working out *(c)* will affect *(a)*, and so on. But *(c)*, the more perceptive of you will have already worked out, is really Practical Criticism. In other words, by studying literature as suggested above you are sharpening your skills of Practical Criticism, and as you do that, you develop your reading skills and make the study of literature more rewarding. And the more we develop reading skills the more our writing skills are affected.

Remember the three questions:

(a) What is the novel/play/poem/film about?

(b) What are its effects on me?

(c) How have these effects been produced?

These questions provide a way into the studying of literature and a structure for the most effective preparation for the examination.

– 2 –

THE LITERATURE PAPER IN HIGHER ENGLISH

There are three elements involved in the assessment of the Revised version of Higher English:

> Folio of Personal Studies
> Paper I
> Paper II

and each one of these elements is externally assessed. In practice, this means that you have to submit a Personal Studies Folio and you have to sit two external papers. All this adds up to 195 marks.

Let us look at this sytem of assessment in more detail.

Folio of Personal Studies

What is meant by *Personal Studies*? The Folio of Personal Studies involves two things: you have to submit to the Board by 31st March of the year you sit the examination:

(a) a Review of Personal Reading (or RPR)   (worth 40 marks)
and

(b) **either** a piece of Imaginative/Personal Writing **or** a piece of Discursive Writing   (worth 25 marks)

(Total 65 marks)

There are also, as has been pointed out, two external papers, papers you sit under examination conditions, and these are:

Paper I — Reading

This paper lasts for 2 hours 5 minutes and consists of two compulsory parts:

Part 1 — Close Reading or Interpretation — there may be one or two passages set, and if there are two, there may be some questions which will ask you to compare and/or contrast the passages . . .   (worth 40 marks)

Part 2 — Report — in this part you will be required to study several related texts and produce a report . . .   (worth 35 marks)

(Total 75 marks)

Paper II — Writing

This paper lasts for 1 hour 35 minutes and also consists of **two** compulsory parts.

In Part 1 there are **two** sections, of which you have to choose one:

Section A — Practical Criticism (which may be a poem, piece of prose, or piece of dramatic dialogue);

Section B — Close Reading of a Specified Text.

(worth 25 marks)

In Part 2 there is a Critical Essay — you will be required to write a critical essay on one of a range of topics relating to literature or the mass media.

(worth 30 marks)

(Total 55 marks)

This book deals with your preparation for the RPR and for Paper II.

As I said, the RPR has to be submitted by March of the year in which you sit the examination, and clearly this means that you have to spend your Higher year preparing for the Folio. Exactly how you should go about this is dealt with in a later chapter, but what you do need to know here is that you have to make a detailed study throughout your Higher course of a single literary (or media) text, or set of short texts. If you choose the latter, you might want to effect a contrast and/or comparison of the texts. You might, however, choose to make a comparison between a literary text and its film or TV version.

Whatever you choose to do, your final submission must be in the form of an extended piece of writing between 1000 and 1500 words in length.

It is also worth noting here that there are certain exclusions that exist with reference to this examination. One of these exclusions prevents you from using the text that is the basis of your RPR anywhere else in the examination. And, if a radio, film or TV script is used for your RPR, you may not choose to answer a question from the Mass Media Section in Paper II, Part 2.

Paper II is, then, the literature paper, though it is not actually called that. It is made up of Practical Criticism, Specified Texts and the Critical Essay.

What is meant by Practical Criticism? Don't worry about the answer to this question at this stage. I shall go into a great deal of detail about Practical

7

Criticism later on; all you need to know at the moment is that in the Practical Criticism question you are given an unseen passage — a poem or a piece of prose or a piece of dramatic dialogue — followed by questions which will ask you about the effects the passage has on you and about how the writer achieves these effects.

Now you ask: *What is meant by Specified Texts?* The Specified Texts section — Section B — will contain a key passage from each of the specified prose or dramatic texts. It will also contain a complete poem, or a key passage from a poem, from each of the specified sets of poems. If you choose to do Section B, you have to attempt the questions on one of these key passages or poems. The questions are designed to test your knowledge and understanding of the passage itself, its immediate context, and its relationship to the text as a whole, or to other poem(s) in the remainder of the set if you have been given an entire poem.

What is meant by the Critical Essay? Again, I shall go over the Critical Essay in a great deal of detail later, but you must know that you have to produce, in this part of the paper, an essay of about 400 – 500 words in length, written in continual formal prose. As well as testing your knowledge, understanding and appreciation of literature, this question also tests your discursive writing skills. Part 2 is in the form of four sections: Section A — Drama; Section B — Prose; Section C — Poetry; Section D — Mass Media. The Mass Media questions deal with specified areas of study, and you will find much more information about it in *A Guide to Mass Media* by E. Thomson (Robert Gibson & Sons, 1991).

This chapter has been a very brief outline of the place of literature in Higher English (Revised). Later chapters will deal with all that has been set out here in much greater detail.

We could progress from here by devoting a chapter to the assessment of literature in the Folio, then to another on the assessment of literature in Paper II, but that would almost be to begin at the end. Success at the end — knowing exactly what to do by March and what to do on the day of the examination — depends on your having acquired the right techniques for studying literature. Therefore we have to go back to the beginning: how do you set about the proper study of literary texts?

– 3 –

TECHNIQUES INVOLVED IN THE STUDY OF LITERATURE

There are various ways of going about the study of literature. All of them depend on an intimate and thorough knowledge of the text you are studying for the exam. One favourite method adopted by too many candidates is to buy one of the many commercially-produced notes on the text and to repeat them in the exam itself: this method is almost guaranteed to lead to a C award at best or disaster at worst. One thing looked for in candidates' responses by examiners is originality and genuineness. If you can get across in your answer an enthusiasm for and an individuality in your ideas about (as well as a thorough-going knowledge of) the text you will do well.

How do you achieve this enthusiasm, this individuality, this genuineness? Not really by studying only what other people think. What matters is what you think of the text. What counts is having your own ideas about *Hamlet*, *Sunset Song* and *Afternoons*. But, you may well, and rightly, ask: how do I go about developing my own ideas? Answer: by developing your skills of Practical Criticism. So that is where we'll begin — with the P.C.

What is Practical Criticism (better known as PC)? Well, it's not just that part of Paper II that the faint-hearted see as the section to be avoided and the idle as the soft option. It is also Part 1 of Paper I, since the close reading questions are often very like PC questions in that they ask about language features and author technique; some of the questions in the Specified Texts are also very close to PC-type questions in that they too ask about language features and how authors manage to create the effects that they do. If you think about it, even if you want to escape Practical Criticism, you can't, But you don't want to escape it anyway: PC is more than a set of questions on a given passage, it is a whole way of approaching literature and the study of literature.

Practical Criticism is a way of helping students to evaluate a text. It is too easy when asked about a new text or television play or film to give a comment that you think is the comment being looked for — the 'correct' comment; equally, it is too easy to give a subjective, uninformed opinion — 'it's all right' or 'it's a load of rubbish'. Practical Criticism is a method of examining the text — what is actually written — very closely in order to arrive at your own informed opinion of how well the author has written it. In other words, your opinion will be objective because it is based on the text, and it will be an expression of what you have got out of the text.

First and foremost, then, Practical Criticism is an examination of what the author has actually said. When you approach a text for the first time you must initially get to know it: read it carefully and become familiar with it. Then ask yourself the three questions:

(a) What is the text about?

(b) What effects did it have on me?

(c) How were these effects achieved?

It is important to be honest in your answers, and to be as aware as you can be of your own reactions. Let's take each question in turn.

(a) *What is the text about?*

You've come across the following situation —

Tracy: "Did you see that new police series last night?"

Dawn: "No I didn't, I missed it. What was it about?"

Tracy: "Well, there was this man, and he had just robbed a bank and as he was running away, he dropped a whole load of cash and . . ."

— and so Tracy drones on, boring Dawn to tears by going over every detail of the programme. We've all of us felt our hearts sink when one of our acquaintances has done the same thing: recounted a play or a film or a book to the death.

The situation would be less irritating if the conversation had to take a slightly different turn —

Tracy: "Did you see that new police series last night?"

Dawn: "No I didn't, I missed it. What was it about?"

Tracy: "Well I suppose it was about inadequacy. A lonely bachelor turned to shoplifting . . ."

and Tracy goes on, briefly, to illustrate the theme of inadequacy by referring to a couple of scenes from the episode.

In the second of the two conversations, Tracy has more idea of what the question "What is the text about?" involves. The answer needs to be in terms of a theme or issue. Thus the question "What is *Hamlet* about?" can have, as one of its answers, "Revenge".

Once you have established in your own mind what you think the text you are studying is about, you are ready to go on to the next question.

(b)   *What effects did it have on me?*

This question really is concerned with your reaction to whatever it is you've been reading or viewing. The printed word has the capacity to make us laugh, cry, feel sad, feel pity, feel happy and even, on occasions, it can make us feel bored. This process is very complex and no-one really understands the psychological factors involved. This is not the book to try and explore these things, but a word has to be said about the more superficial aspects of how we react to a book, play or poem.

Let's begin with how it is an author comes to write a book. Obviously, it is impossible to plumb the depths of any author's psyche to find out what demon has driven him to fill a page with writing — this author doesn't even want anyone to begin to find out — but something can be said about the process. All authors really do write from experience, but unlike the rest of us they are really very acutely aware of their own experience. They reflect on it, analyse it, dissect it. They also have a heightened sensitivity, together, obviously, with developed articulacy — they can use words. Words become the tools the author uses to re-create those experiences; the novel, the play, the poem becomes the symbolic representation of his experiences. Maybe the following diagram will help you understand:

author   book

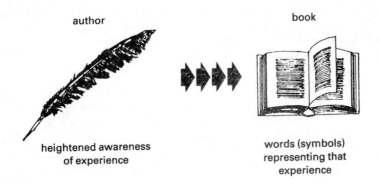

heightened awareness   words (symbols)
of experience   representing that
                                           experience

Now experience, by definition, is private to each individual. The only way we can "share" experience is by talking about it: that is, we have to use words.

An author is doing the same thing only more skilfully, and he is deliberately trying to re-create the experience itself. When we read what he has written we have to rely on our own experiences — since experience is private. We bring our experiences to the printed word and allow the words to re-pattern the experiences we have already undergone.

So you could say that the reading process is the writing process in reverse. Again, a diagram might make it easier to understand:

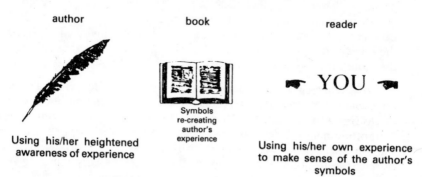

author   book   reader

Symbols
re-creating
author's
experience

➤ YOU ➤

Using his/her heightened
awareness of experience

Using his/her own experience
to make sense of the author's
symbols

In other words the author, in a work of art, isn't communicating directly with the reader: he depends on the reader's own experiences and, to a large extent, he re-patterns, re-organises the reader's experiences. Now if the reader has limited experience, or is unaware of his experiences, then that reader will become easily bored with what the author has written. The author will be making demands of the reader which the reader is unable to meet. Similarly, of course, the reader can make demands of a text which the author is unable to meet — the text can be too simplistic and dull!

So when I say we should be aware of the effects a text has on us, I am saying that we should be aware of our experience being re-worked, re-patterned, re-organised by the text. All we can bring to a text is our experience, and our understanding of that text will be in terms of that experience. Obviously intelligence, imagination and our own facility with words all play a part, but in the main, our concern is with experience. As our experience changes, develops, as we mature, our relationship with the text will change, develop, mature. What we feel when we read *Ode to a Nightingale* at 18 years of age won't be what we feel when we read the same poem at 38 years of age.

Let me give you a concrete example. Take Kevin, aged 44. He can still remember his Higher English course: it consisted of *L'Allegro*, *Il Pensoroso*, *The History of Mr. Polly* and *Hamlet*. It was, quite simply, awful. He had notes dictated to him about what each of these texts "meant", and he was told what to say about each of them. He was bored. His friends all seemed satisfied with this meagre diet. Then one dull wet Saturday in the middle of an Edinburgh winter he re-read *Hamlet*, this time on his terms. Suddenly the play became alive and three-dimensional: it wasn't about revenge or procrastination any longer. It was about an intelligent, sensitive, articulate young man who was surrounded by thickies. He knew how Hamlet felt! The play wasn't, after all, some geometric theorem to be learned by heart and spouted out under exam conditions: it was about himself. He knew how Hamlet felt in his opening scene: dressed in black to mark himself out from the rest — the gaudily dressed, the insensitive, the superficial, the easily satisfied.

That Saturday taught Kevin something about the nature of literature that no English teacher had ever managed to teach him. Literature could be alive and personal and about how he, himself, felt — in other words it could be about experience and not about a set of dictated notes. Needless to say Kevin grew up: *Hamlet* no longer strikes him in that way; it now accords with all kinds of experiences he has gained since the age of 17. In other words, his relationship with the play has altered, but only because he has changed over the years.

I hope you see what I am getting at. Use your experience when you read, and don't be afraid of your reactions, if they are your honest reactions.

The intellectually demanding question is: how have these reactions been brought about? We've now come to question *(c)*, which is the business of Practical Criticism.

(c)   *How were these effects achieved?*
How has the author put the text together? What techniques has the author used to create the effects he has achieved?

Literature is art and like all art it is artificially constructed — it is designed and put together by someone in a particular and definite way. Therefore it is quite possible, with a great deal of skill, to examine how it has been put together; that is the function of Practical Criticism and the job of students of all literary forms. That may seem to you almost a

13

cold-hearted and destructive thing to do, like a scientist dispassionately dissecting tissue. But it is not really like that: literature, especially poetry, often deals with very complex emotions, attitudes and experiences in a way so compressed as to render it immediately inaccessible to a reader — it is unlikely that you will discover all that there is to discover in a poem at first or even tenth reading. You need to make an effort to gain a fuller understanding, and the analysis of the techniques the author has used, far from destroying his art, should enhance it and allow the work to make its fullest impact on you.

What sorts of techniques do we need to know about? Obviously they differ according to the text itself: a novel will demand a knowledge of setting and characterisation, a play of plot, staging and lighting, a poem of verse structure and rhythm — though, of course, there is overlap. But you need above all to have a knowledge of language and the way it works. And you need to know something about structure.

– 4 –

LANGUAGE AND THE WAY IT WORKS

"Grammar" is the term we give to the way in which words form a recognisable pattern. For example, you instantly recognise the following arrangement of words:

> *I went into the café and bought a Coke.*

You would still recognise the following re-arrangement:

> *Into the café I went and bought a Coke*

or even:

> *Into the café I went and a Coke I bought*

but you would have difficulty with:

> *A into Coke the Café I went bought I and.*

There are, then, rules of grammar which govern the way in which we arrange words to make that arrangement meaningful. The rules are to do with the connections between words and the function of each word in the sentence. We label the words as follows — and it is important to realise that for the Revised Higher you need to know these labels:

Verbs — words which relate to actions
> (e.g.: I **went** to the docks and **saw** the Tall Ships.)

Nouns — the names of things or persons
> (e.g.: The **boy** ate the **orange** outside the **disco**.)

Pronouns — words which stand for nouns
> (e.g.: **He** ate **it** outside the disco.)

Prepositions — words such as to, for, into, below
> (e.g.: I went **into** the cupboard **beneath** the stairs.)

Adjectives — words which describe nouns
> (e.g.: The **clever young** girl scored an A in Higher English.)

Articles — the, a
> (e.g.: **The** dog ate **a** biscuit from **the** bag.)

15

Adverbs — words which modify/affect the meaning of a verb
  (e.g.: The ship **slowly** but **surely** sank in the river.)

Present participles — verbs which end in -ing
  (e.g.: **Turning** and **turning** in the **widening** gyre.)

The rules allow only a certain order of words — you can say *into the* but not *the into*. Now the point of all this is that when the words are in a meaningful arrangement then there is a meaningful context — the terms are laid down by which we can work out the meaning of any given word. For example,

I reached the bar where I was to have a drink with my friend.

We know by linking " drink" with "bar" that the "bar" isn't a wall bar in a gym. Further, we know that the "drink" in this example probably isn't a Coke.

All of us can operate these rules without being aware of them, but for the purpose of Practical Criticism we need to become aware of the rules. The meaning of a word in a sentence, then, is determined by its relationship with the other words in the sentence.

The other thing you need to know is that words have two levels of meaning — denotation and connotation. The denotation of a word is the actual "thing" to which the word refers. If I say "There's my dog chasing that cat" then the denotation of "dog" is my actual dog and the denotation of "cat" is the actual cat my dog is chasing. The connotation of a word is the picture conjured up in our mind by our associations with the particular word and our experiences of it.

Look carefully at the following list of words, or better still give the book to someone else and get him or her to read out the list slowly to you. Have a pencil and paper handy, and as you hear each word jot down whatever comes into your head. Don't spend time thinking of an answer, just jot down a word as it comes into your mind.

Bottle	Apple
Fire	Car
School	Sea
Girl	Book
Bar	Food.

Now against "Bottle" you might have written "milk", "glass", "green", "whisky" or even "ship". None of these responses is wrong — each is for the person who thought of the response the connotative area of the word. Look carefully at all ten of *your* words — these are for you the connotations of each

16

of the ten words above. Again, although all ten words are in our language, and are therefore shared by all of us, each connotation is unique and private: each connotation depends on your experiences of and associations with the word.

Poetry operates at the level of connotation. When we read a poem we should allow our imaginations to work on the words and images so that we are aware of the connotations. For example,

"His secret murders sticking on his hands." (*Macbeth*)

Think of what "sticking" suggests to you, and think of what the idea of a murder sticking to someone's hands suggests.

But also remember what I said about the rules of language and how the meaning of one word is affected/determined by the meaning of other words in the same sentence. Although poetry operates at the level of connotation, nevertheless the area of connotation of a word is limited by the meaning of that word within the context of the sentence. Take another example,

"The star-eaten blanket of the sky."

That image may appear meaningless or, indeed, it may cause our imaginations to run riot, producing in us a kind of startled awareness because of its freshness. But given that the line appears in a poem about a tramp sleeping on the Embankment, and gives the association of "star-eaten" with "moth-eaten" then the meaning of the line becomes clearer.

In other words, although I say you cannot be wrong when you respond to "bottle" with "milk", nevertheless you cannot make just any response to a word or image in a poem: you have to take account of the meaning of such a word as defined by the overall context.

Meaning, then, has to do with the structure of a sentence and the connotative areas of words within that sentence, though the two are obviously incredibly closely linked and the one affects the other. For example, contrast

"I walked into the classroom and I saw the overturned desks, the broken chairs, the waste paper on the floor and the writing on the wall."

with

"I walked into the classroom and I saw the overturned desks and the broken chairs and the waste paper on the floor and the writing on the wall."

17

The difference between the two sentences is one of structure: the first is a list in conventional form with the "and" between the last two items, whereas the second sentence uses "and" between each item. But what difference does that make? The first list is in haphazard order — you can interchange the items without really affecting meaning. But in the second the "and" suggests that each item is linked to the one which has gone before in a significant way: "writing on the wall" takes on almost a metaphorical meaning, as though some disaster is implied by the gradual build-up. In other words, the structure with the conjunctions (polysyndetic structure) suggests or connotes something sinister in a way in which the structure without the conjunctions (asyndetic structure) doesn't.

Take the following extract, from the opening of *Under Milk Wood*, a play by Dylan Thomas, and let's examine some of the structures:

UNDER MILK WOOD
[*Silence*]
FIRST VOICE (*Very softly*)

To begin at the beginning:

It is spring, moonless night in the small town, starless and bible-black, the cobblestreets silent and the hunched, courters'-and-rabbits' wood limping invisible down to the sloeblack, slow, black, crowblack, fishingboat-bobbing sea. The houses are blind as moles (though moles see fine to-night in the snouting, velvet dingles) or blind as Captain Cat there in the muffled middle by the pump and the town clock, the shops in mourning, the Welfare Hall in widows' weeds. And all the people of the lulled and dumbfound town are sleeping now.

Hush, the babies are sleeping, the farmers, the fishers, the tradesmen and pensioners, cobbler, school-teacher, postman and publican, the undertaker and the fancy woman, drunkard, dressmaker, preacher, policeman, the webfoot cocklewomen and the tidy wives. Young girls lie bedded soft or glide in their dreams, with rings and trousseaux, bridesmaided by glow-worms down the aisles of the organplaying wood. The boys are dreaming wicked or of the bucking ranches of the night and the jollyrodgered sea. And the anthracite statues of the horses sleep in the fields, and the cows in the byres, and the dogs in the wetnosed yards; and the cats nap in the slant corners or lope sly, streaking and needling, on the one cloud of the roofs.

You can hear the dew falling, and the hushed town breathing. Only *your* eyes are unclosed to see the black and folded town fast, and slow, asleep. And you alone can hear the invisible starfall, the darkest-before-dawn minutely dewgrazed stir of the black, dab-filled sea where the *Arethusa*, the *Curlew* and the *Skylark*, *Zanzibar*, *Rhiannon*, the *Rover*, the *Cormorant*, and the *Star of Wales* tilt and ride.

Listen. It is night moving in the streets, the processional salt slow musical wind in Coronation Street and Cockle Row, it is the grass growing on Llaregyb Hill, dewfall, starfall, the sleep of birds in Milk Wood.

Listen. It is night in the chill, squat chapel, hymning in bonnet and brooch and bombazine black, butterfly choker and bootlace bow, coughing like nannygoats, sucking mintoes, fortywinking hallelujah; night in the four-ale, quiet as a domino; in Ocky Milkman's lofts like a mouse with gloves; in Dai Bread's bakery flying like black flour. It is tonight in Donkey Street, trotting silent, with seaweed on its hooves, along the cockled cobbles, past curtained fernpot, text and trinket, harmonium, holy dresser, watercolours done by hand, china dog and rosy tin teacaddy. It is night neddying among the snuggeries of babies.

Look. It is night, dumbly, royally winding through the Coronation cherry trees; going through the graveyard of Bethesda with winds gloved and folded, and dew doffed; tumbling by the Sailors Arms.

Time passes. Listen. Time passes.

From *Under Milk Wood* by Dylan Thomas.

Note for a start, the author's use of the list —

(a)   . . . limping invisible down to the sloeblack, slow, black, fishing-boat bobbing sea.

(b)   . . . the babies are sleeping, the farmers, the fishers, the tradesmen and pensioners, cobbler, school-teacher, postman and publican, the undertaker and the fancy woman, drunkard, dressmaker, preacher, policeman, the webfoot cocklewomen and the tidy wives.

See if you can find another list in the extract.

What structure are these lists in — polysyndetic or asyndetic?

We've talked about the connotations of words and how the context guides us as to which of the connotations or word pictures is the most appropriate. Look at the beginning of the extract:

> It is spring, moonless night in the small town, starless and bible-black.

Thomas uses three words to create and intensify the darkness: "moonless", "starless" and "bible-black". "Bible-black" seems odd, but given that the play is set in a Welsh village which is very religious — almost repressively religious — then the connotations of "bible-black" become clearer — it's not just a colour image, but suggests the attitudes of the inhabitants.

Dylan Thomas uses this technique a great deal. Many of the words he uses or even makes up make little sense outwith the context he creates. Once we grasp the context, we can understand what he is doing with the words:

(a)   ". . . the boys are dreaming . . . of the bucking ranches of the night and the jollyrodgered sea."

"bucking" isn't normally used to describe ranches, and he has made up the word "jollyrodgered", but you can see that both words are appropriate within the context.

(b)   "And the anthracite statues of the horses sleep in the fields . . . and the dogs in the wetnosed yards."

Again the horses are not statues made of anthracite, and he has made up the word "wetnosed" — but you can see why.

Can you find any other examples such as these?

On page 16, I mentioned present participles: the bit of the verb that ends in -ing. Note how often Thomas uses such words in this extract. "streaking and needling", "dew falling", "hushed town breathing", "night moving" — there are many, many examples. What is the effect of all this? Present participles not only stress movement, they suggest the action is happening now — in the present — and is happening continuously. And that is exactly the effect the dramatist is after as the speaker invites the audience to listen to and look at all that is happening as dawn breaks over the village.

So far we have looked at grammar and word-order, denotation and connotation, and context. What other techniques are open to a writer? We have to come back to the word "structure". Just as a writer structures a sentence in order to create a certain effect, he has also to structure the whole piece he has written. He will structure paragraphs, chapters, the whole novel; in a play he will build acts and scenes into the structure he wants; and in poetry he will use lines, verses and/or verse-paragraphs. We'll go into this in more detail when we look more closely at the novel, the drama and poetry. Meanwhile it's enough to draw your attention to the fact that all texts — even short extracts — have a structure. The extract from *Under Milk Wood* (see page 18) has its own structure. It opens with a wide view of the town, sketching in a few general details, then (much as the opening of a film might do) it moves in more closely looking at intricate detail. Note the use of "Listen" and "Look" and the points at which these words come in the speech — that's also part of the structure. If I tell you that the play was originally written for radio, can you then detect anything in the structure that might make it more appropriate for radio, than for, say, television?

The next sets of techniques that you need to know something about are the techniques of RHYTHM and SOUND. Rhythm and sound are closely related and they are devices not exclusive to poetry. However, let's begin with poetry and, in particular, with *The Castle* by Edwin Muir.

THE CASTLE

All through that summer at ease we lay,
And daily from the turret wall
We watched the mowers in the hay
And the enemy half a mile away.
They seemed no threat to us at all.

For what, we thought, had we to fear
With our arms and provender, load on load,
Our towering battlements, tier or tier,
And friendly allies drawing near
On every leafy summer road.

Our gates were strong, our walls were thick,
So smooth and high, no man could win
A foothold there, no clever trick
Could take us, have us dead or quick.
Only a bird could have got in.

What could they offer us for bait?
Our captain was brave and we were true . . .
There was a little private gate,
A little wicked wicket gate.
The wizened warder let them through.

21

Oh then our maze of tunnelled stone
Grew thin as treacherous as air.
The cause was lost without a groan,
The famous citadel overthrown,
And all its secret galleries bare.

How can this shameful tale be told?
I will maintain until my death
We could do nothing, being sold;
Our only enemy was gold,
And we had no arms to fight it with.

From *The Collected Poems* of Edwin Muir.

Now rhythm is very much a matter of the sound of the words chosen. The sound of a word depends on the vowel sounds and the consonants. In English there are five vowels: a, e, i, o and u. These vowels can be either *short* or *long*. For example —

short	a	ă pronounced as in	*hat*
long	a	ā pronounced as in	*hate*
short	e	ĕ pronounced as in	*pet*
long	e	ē pronounced as in	*Pete*
short	i	ĭ pronounced as in	*lit*
long	i	ī pronounced as in	*light*
short	o	ŏ pronounced as in	*dot*
long	o	ō pronounced as in	*dote*

Short vowel sounds tend to be said quickly and long vowel sounds slowly. Certain consonants also create speed — *t d*; some create violent sounds — *b p*; others slow words down — *w l m n y*; others create a hissing sound which can be used in a variety of ways — *s z*.

Let's look at the opening stanza of *The Castle*:

All through that summer at ease we lay,
And daily from the turret wall
We watched the mowers in the hay
And the enemy half a mile away.
They seemed no threat to us at all.

Note the number of long vowel sounds: "through", "ease", "lay", "daily", "mowers", "hay", "mile", "away", "seemed". Note also the consonants that slow words down: the double *ll* in *all*, the *s* and *m* of *summer*, the *s* of *ease*, the *l* of *lay*, the *l* and *y* of *daily*, the double *ll* of *wall*, the *w* of *we* and *watched*; even getting the tongue round the *t, ch* and *d* of *watched* helps to slow down the pace.

Now when you examine what the author is actually saying, you can see how the long, slow moving sentence contributes to those feelings of languor and security. The last line speeds up considerably (short vowel sounds and fast-sounding consonants) and, combined with the word 'seemed', gives the suggestion that the security is perhaps false.

You can go through the second and third stanzas yourself, but note the cumulative effect of "load on load" and "tier on tier". But let's examine the fourth stanza:

> What cōuld thēȳ offer us for bāīt?
> Our captāīn was brāve and wē were trūē . . .
> There wăs a lĭttle private gate,
> A lĭttle wĭckĕd wĭckĕt gate.
> The wĭzĕned wărdĕr lĕt thĕm through.

We can say a great deal about rhythm and sound and its contribution to meaning. That isn't quite right: I've been suggesting that sound *contributes* to meaning, as though somehow the two are separate — not so, sound is part of the meaning. However, you can see from the long/short distribution above that the first two lines are made up of long vowel sounds and the next three of short vowel sounds. You can see why: the first two are the culmination of the security built up at the beginning of the poem, whereas the lines after the three dots suddenly and effectively expose the security for what it was — false. Listen to the nasty *ĭ* sounds in *little, wicked, wicket, wizened*. The nasty short ĭ sound is preceded by the mean *w* sound: even to form the *w* you have to pull the lips together making the mouth narrow and mean-looking! You cannot escape noticing the repetition of this *w* — we call the repetition of a consonant *alliteration*.

In the passing, it is worth commenting on the structure of this verse, already mentioned above. The first two lines form the climax of the build-up of security — the first line is a question which implies its own answer (we call that a *rhetorical question*) and the second makes a statement that is almost a cliché: captains are always brave and the troops are always true. The interesting point is the use of the three dots after "true . . ." we read the next three lines almost without realising what has happened. The castle is taken by a means not at all expected and the three dots are a means by which we, the reader, are taken in unexpectedly. It is also worth commenting on the last word of the third and fourth line: the word "gate" is repeated, whereas elsewhere in the poem the last words of the third and fourth lines merely rhyme. Again this is a technique by which the author draws attention to his meaning. Only after reading this verse are we aware of the irony running through the earlier part of the poem — but more will be said about irony later.

Another important aspect of sound is *onomatopoeia*, where the sound of a word is closely related to the meaning. In *The Castle* there are several onomatopœic words — "ease", "groan", and, as has been already suggested, even a word such as "wicked".

Rhyme is, of course, what everyone thinks of when poetry is mentioned. To work out a poem's rhyme scheme use the alphabet and repeat a letter at each rhyme, thus:

All through that summer at ease we lay,	*a*
And daily from the turret wall	*b*
We watched the mowers in the hay	*a*
And the enemy half a mile away.	*a*
They seemed no threat to us at all	*b*

This *a b a a b* pattern creates a very compact verse with the last line standing out yet echoing the second line. The rhyme gives the poem an eerie yet romantic feel. Look again at the last verse:

How can this shameful tale be told?	*a*
I will maintain until my death	*b*
We could do nothing, being sold;	*a*
Our only enemy was gold,	*a*
And we had no arms to fight it with.	*b*

But, you claim, this time the second and last lines don't rhyme. Well, they do and they don't, if you know what I mean! And you are right — the lines nearly rhyme, and we call that device para-rhyme. It's not that the poet couldn't be bothered to find a rhyming word — he deliberately nearly rhymes the words to create a kind of ghostly, echoing, but almost sad effect. But Muir here breaks all kinds of rules: he ends not only a line, not only a sentence, but the whole poem with a preposition. It has always been considered (wrongly, of course) that to end a sentence with a preposition indicates either a poor education or bad taste on the part of a writer. Churchill, somewhat tongue-in-cheek, claimed "That is something up with which I shall not put" to avoid such a stylistic faux-pas! Muir deliberately ends with 'with', so altering the rhythm of the line that he breaks the eerie, romantic feel and creates a very 20th century feel instead. The very limpness of the line contrasts with the kind of mediaeval imagery of the rest of the poem, and that limpness, that afterthought, makes us realise that the poem isn't just about romantic castles of yesteryear but is also about greed and how all of us, including society as a whole, can be bought — for the right price.

One final point about rhythm and sound when it comes to poetry: the use of the line. One of the big differences between poetry and prose (this book is written in prose) is that poetry is written in lines. Often the line stands by itself — the break at the end of the line sounds quite natural because it's part of the structure not only of the poem but of the sentence. Look again at *The Castle*: almost all the lines stand by themselves. Verse one is like this, as is verse two: the grammatical structure fits the line structure. But note verse three, lines two and three:

> So smooth and high, no man could win
> A foothold there, no clever trick
> Could take us, have us dead or quick.

Here you can see that the grammatical structure does not quite fit the line structure: "A foothold there" spills over on to the next line, as does "could take us". Again, this is a deliberate device called *enjambement* or *run-on-lines* which usually creates tension in a poem, because the grammatical structure is being forced into the verse/line structure without quite fitting it. Some poets use this device to quite startling effect.

We have examined a great deal in this chapter and you may well have to read it and re-read it several times. The important thing to remember is that when you are studying literature the last thing you want to do is to learn up notes — you should approach the texts you are studying through the three questions set out on page 10:

(a) What is the text about?
(b) What effects did it have on me?
(c) How were these effects achieved?

and this chapter has been very much concerned with question *(c)*. And that applies to whichever of the two Highers you are working for — the principle remains unaltered.

Now we must turn to the three genres of literature: drama, prose and poetry and look at each in turn. For Media Studies see *A Guide to the Mass Media*.

– 5 –

DRAMA

Drama forms a vital and important part of any course on literature. Perhaps we should go back to basics and examine the nature of drama. There are various terms we use: "theatre", "the theatre", "drama", "the drama", "stage", "play". Each of these words means something quite distinct. A stage is really a lit area. Imagine, for example, you are walking home from school one dark winter's evening along a street of semi-detached houses. You pass by one house — the living room is lit and the curtains are open. You can see in quite easily. Do you stop, just for a look? Of course you do. The lit window is like a cinema or television screen.

As you watch you notice a young lady comes into the room, wearing a chic, black, backless dress. She walks up to the mantlepiece and lifts a glass of champagne and stands there with her back to the room. Still interested? The door opens again and in walks a young man; he walks up to her, but obviously she is unaware of his presence. He pulls a long knife from his dinner jacket and takes one more step . . .

By this point you are riveted. You have before you all the ingredients of a drama, set on a lit stage: sex, violence but above all conflict. What gets your attention is the lit area; the movement helps to keep your attention. These two ingredients alone can halt the most fascinating of conversations: there is nothing quite like a TV set switched on high up in a corner of a pub to hold the attention of an open-mouthed crowd stunned into silence by News at Ten with the sound off.

No matter how absorbed you are in this book your attention could easily be distracted by the tip-toeing of a little mouse as it crosses the floor in front of your chair. Movement is a vital ingredient of drama and theatre.

But to keep your attention there has to be conflict. All the plays you know, the films you have seen, the soap operas you couldn't miss are all based on conflict. Just count the conflict in any of your favourite soap operas at the moment. Usually the conflict is external — Goodies –v– Baddies, Cowboys –v– Indians, Cops –v– Villains. Often those in conflict are dressed in easily identified uniforms to make the conflict recognisable. The characters involved are simple, almost two-dimensional, cardboard cut-outs. The values involved are stark: the good are very good and the bad are wicked.

More complex dramas begin to involve complications — the good aren't always that good and even the baddie can have admirable qualities. Sometimes the dramatist introduces conflict within the hero himself — what we call internal conflict. Much of the drama you are studying for Higher English will involve internal conflict — as well as, of course, external conflict. Hamlet is not only in conflict with Claudius, but is in conflict with himself: part of him wants to revenge his father's murder, but another part of him recognises the futility of revenge. Macbeth isn't only in conflict with Malcolm and Macduff; he also recognises the futility of his existence and the pointlessness of what he is doing. Willy Loman is in conflict with Biff on the one hand and with the American Dream on the other; but he is also torn internally by his love of the great outdoors and physical labour, and by his ambition to achieve success and fame in the city.

Conflict, then, is the basis of all drama, and the conflict is both external and internal. Your study of plays should begin with an examination of conflict. We call the characters working for good the *protagonists* and the forces in conflict with the protagonists we call the *antagonistic forces*. Begin by making a list of the protagonists and of the antagonistic forces. In complex drama the task isn't easy because some characters may well fit into both lists — but try it for the texts you are studying. You also have to bear in mind that antagonistic forces are not always characters: Hamlet is in conflict with the social and moral values of the time; John Proctor is in conflict with the values of the society of which he is a part.

Once you have worked out who is in conflict with whom or with what, you should work out the nature of the conflict: what is the cause of it, how is it expressed, in what ways does it come to a climax, how is the conflict resolved?

There can be many factors which contribute to the conflict, and it can be a complicated job working out the various strands involved. For example, the final major conflict in *Hamlet* is between the mighty opposites Hamlet and

27

Claudius, though, of course, that conflict runs through the whole play. But examine the strands that contribute to that conflict and intensify it:

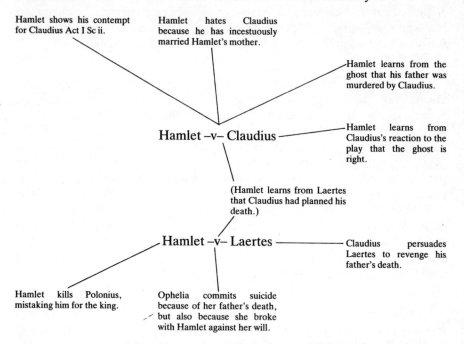

Hamlet shows his contempt for Claudius Act I Sc ii.

Hamlet hates Claudius because he has incestuously married Hamlet's mother.

Hamlet learns from the ghost that his father was murdered by Claudius.

Hamlet –v– Claudius

Hamlet learns from Claudius's reaction to the play that the ghost is right.

(Hamlet learns from Laertes that Claudius had planned his death.)

Hamlet –v– Laertes

Claudius persuades Laertes to revenge his father's death.

Hamlet kills Polonius, mistaking him for the king.

Ophelia commits suicide because of her father's death, but also because she broke with Hamlet against her will.

Conflict is, as has been stressed, the basis of drama, but all drama also involves issues or themes. Remember I said that after you've read a text you should ask yourself what it is about? The answer to that question — and there can be a few answers to the question — gives you the theme — or themes — of the play. Once you have read the text and analysed the conflict as suggested above, you should spend some time thinking out the themes — thinking out what it is the play says to you. Write down the themes or issues you have decided on, then go back to the text to see which scenes establish the theme or illustrate it or develop it. One of the major themes in *Macbeth* is duplicity — appearances are deceptive, the underlying reality is dangerous, often fatal, and belies the apparently innocent surface:

> "Look like the innocent flower, but be the serpent under it."

> "False face must hide what the false heart doth know."

"This castle hath a pleasant seat", says Duncan, little realising it is to be the seat of his assassination. But how does this theme get established in the play? Look carefully at Act I Scene i and examine what the witches say: "Fair is foul and foul is fair" and then look at the first words spoken by

28

Macbeth. As you go through the play you will find many instances where the theme of duplicity is reinforced, and as you find them you should note them down.

But of course there are many themes in the plays that you are likely to be studying for Higher English. Most of these themes are well known, but you may detect in your favourite play themes that other people haven't written about: all that matters is that you can justify whatever theme you want to write about with evidence from the text. The same applies to your opinion of the characters. You may well believe that Hamlet is a moody, spoiled, self-centred little brat who, because his comfortable little world is upset by his mother's remarriage, tries to make life difficult for his stepfather, hoping his interference will end it all. This isn't a conventional view, but it is one which could be sustained by a careful reading of the play. Equally, Hamlet can be thought of as an intelligent intellectual whose integrity and moral values are ahead of and out of step with the times in which he lives. While the others, such as Laertes and Fortinbras, accept the simplistic revenge-philosophy of the time, Hamlet questions the concept of revenge itself. Again this view can be supported by the text. You make up your mind what you think as long as you can back up what you think from your knowledge of the play.

Your study of a play, then, must include a study of conflict, a working-out of themes, an informed knowledge of the characters. All this takes time and effort, and has to be done well in advance of the examination, ideally at the time you are reading the texts in class.

In addition to all this, you should work your way through the following assignment sheet, the answers to which will provide you with your own notes for revision before the exam.

(a) Name the main characters, and the minor ones.

(b) What is the nature of the conflict in the play?

(c) Is the chief/main character involved in any kind of internal conflict, conflict within himself?

(d) What is the outcome of the conflict and how is it arrived at?

(e) What are the themes of the play? (Jealousy, ambition, envy, revenge, unrequited love, duplicity, ingratitude, etcetera.)

(f) How are these themes established/developed/illustrated? (Think in terms of characters and scenes.)

(g)   How well does the opening act introduce us to plot, setting, character, theme, etcetera?

(h)   Did you genuinely enjoy the play? Why? Pick out aspects you especially enjoyed.

(i)   What do you feel you learned from studying the play?

This has been a long chapter and it has asked you to do many things. If you do all that it has asked, then you will be well prepared not only for the examination itself but for the Review of Personal Reading as well — and remember that that is worth 40 marks alone. After all, unlike many candidates **you** may choose to do a piece of drama for your RPR, and if you do, this chapter will have helped you quite considerably.

We have examined drama in much detail, we've gone back to basics and asked ourselves what drama is all about. I want to do the same for Prose and Poetry, then we shall look at the application of what you have learned from this chapter (and from the next two) to the RPR and the examination itself.

Success here, as in everything in life, has to do with the amount of preparation you put in: we **must** spend time on preparing **how** to **study** drama, prose, poetry and media, before we go on to look at how you answer the questions set in the examination.

The next chapter, Chapter 6, will look at Prose. Since the vast majority of candidates tackle prose for the RPR, then perhaps it needs to be read with extreme care.

– 6 –

PROSE

Of all the genres in literature, prose is perhaps unique. Drama is something which is performed and requires actors and an audience; poetry, too, is often performed, and benefits from a group discussion; but prose, particularly the novel, is entirely a private experience. The reader enters imaginatively and therefore privately into the world of the novel, re-creating all that has been set before him or her by the novelist. Another aspect of the novel that makes it different is the sheer size of it: a play lasts for no more than two and a half hours, a poem can take only a few minutes to read, and each is often experienced at one sitting, so to speak. But the novel can take several days to read, has to be picked up and put down, and can, consequently, be difficult to "contain" in the imagination. That also makes it difficult to teach and even more difficult to study: which is why teachers often break up the novel into constituent elements such as "plot", "characterisation", "setting", etcetera.

But first a word about the word "prose". You know what a page of drama looks like with characters on the left, stage instructions in brackets, the words spoken as dialogue; poetry is written in lines and verses; prose is almost anything left over — blocks of print where line endings are of no importance and which contain words which may or may not be spoken. If the words are spoken they are punctuated by direct speech marks called inverted commas. Prose can be the text book you are using in geography, mathematics or science, the newspaper or magazine you read on the bus, the essay you are studying in English. It can also be the novel you have currently taken out from the library. In other words prose can be either prose non-fiction or prose fiction. Prose fiction concerns any prose work which is imaginatively written, which creates a world which does not exist (though it may be based on one which does) and which involves characters which aren't real, but are "made up". Prose non-fiction concerns the real world or the world of facts; it may be a piece recalling events which have occurred; or it may be a reflective piece where the author gives his opinion on events or people or places. Perhaps the easiest way to remember the difference is to bear in mind that novels and short stories are *fiction*, whereas essays, pieces of journalism, travel books are *non-fiction*.

We shall begin with fiction, particularly the novel. Your literature course for either Revised or Unrevised Higher must contain a study of one or more novels, and the question, as with drama, is "what is the best way of tackling the text?" Again go back to the first of the three questions — *(a)* What is the text about? — the answer to which provides you with the theme or themes. As with drama, this isn't an easy task — you need to spend quite a bit of time thinking out what the issues in the novel are for you. Once you've done that and written down the themes, you need to go back to the text to see how the theme is established, which scenes (or incidents) illustrate it, and what part the characters play in the development of it.

One of the major themes in *The Power and The Glory* by Graham Greene, for example, is the conflict between militaristic atheism and corrupt Christianity. That theme is established in a number of ways — the very use of the un-named Lieutenant and Whisky Priest who are symbolic of the two forces involved. But what is really fascinating is the way in which Greene introduces the reader to these characters: the Whisky Priest in Chapter 1 is seen as seedy, shabby, alcoholic, corrupt — but his compassion prevents him from escaping; the Lieutenant is cold, efficient, desperate to introduce to his State equality, fraternity, justice — but he lacks compassion. The Lieutenant is "the little dapper figure of hate carrying his secret of love". The Lieutenant is constantly compared to a priest — "something priest-like", "his monastic cell", his desire to teach the little children — and the priest is the one whose flesh is weak. You should trace these ideas as you read the text. There are other themes in this complex novel, too, of course — and you should try to think them out for yourself.

You need also to know about the characters in the novel you are studying. How are they introduced? How are they developed? Do they learn from experience?

You also have to have some knowledge of the structure of the novel — how it has been put together by the novelist, what setting has been chosen? Why? What is the relationship between setting and plot, and between setting and character? What role does time play in the development of the plot? But, as well as that, you need to study how the novel has been built up — what are the key scenes? How do they advance the plot? How do they affect the outcome?

In *The Power and The Glory* the key central scene must be the one in jail where the Whisky Priest comes upon all of humanity: the prison cell is the microcosm of the world. The contrast is also made between himself, with his alcoholism, illegitimate child, and his state of mortal sin, and the pious woman, with her state of grace but also with her martyrish outlook and utter self-righteousness. Then at the end of the scene the Whisky Priest comes face to face with the Lieutenant for the second time, and for the second time the Lieutenant fails to recognise him. Obviously, there is a great deal more to the scene than that, but it fulfils several functions — it allows Greene an opportunity to make several observations about human attitudes and to comment incisively on the hypocrisy of certain religious people's views.

When we read a novel we can stop at a particular bit we like and think about it. It may be a point at which a character is introduced, or where two characters are in conflict or where the writer seems to halt the narrative in order to comment; or it may, quite simply, be a piece of description which sets a scene or symbolises some aspect of the plot. The point is we can savour such a "moment" in a way in which we can't while watching a film or play. We can think of such a scene in terms of itself, in terms of its immediate context and in terms of the novel as a whole. Indeed such a task is no bad practice for the set text question, since that is exactly the kind of exercise the set text question involves!

In addition to all this you need to work your way through the following assignment sheet which fits all novels and the answers to which will provide you with your own notes for revision before the exam.

Novel Assignment Sheet

(a)   Who tells the story? (Chief character in the first person / minor character in the first person / author in the third person / any other means.)

(b)   What are the advantages of the chosen method of telling the story?

(c)   What type of novel is it? (Fantasy, thriller, science fiction, crime, etcetera.)

(d)   Name the main characters, and the minor ones.

(e)   What is the nature of conflict in the novel?

(f)   Is the chief/main character involved in any kind of internal conflict?

(g)   What is the outcome of the conflict and how is it arrived at?

(h)   What are the themes of the novel? (Jealousy, ambition, envy, revenge, unrequited love, duplicity, ingratitude, etcetera.)

(i)   How are these themes established/developed/illustrated? (Think in terms of characters, scenes, plot, setting.)

(j)   How well does the opening chapter/pages introduce us to plot, setting, character, theme, etcetera?

(k)   Did you genuinely enjoy the novel? Why? Pick out one or two aspects you especially enjoyed.

(l)   What do you feel you learned from studying the novel?

The short story is also part of prose fiction. Familiarity with a short story must include familiarity with the form of the short story, and more nonsense is perhaps written about the short story form than about any other aspect of literature. Candidates still trot out the importance of the "twist in the tail" when some of the best short stories display no such quirk. What distinguishes the short story from the novel is its "single-mindedness": it concerns itself with one idea, and all that the short story contains — language, setting, characterisation, atmosphere — is geared to the deployment of that idea. What characterises the short story is its economy — nothing is wasted, nothing is extra, everything counts, everything is pared down to the bare essentials: and it all goes towards what it is the author wants to say, to depict, to illustrate. Everything is focused very sharply. And all that contrasts with the novel, which by its nature is diffuse, wide-ranging.

If you are going to study a short story for the exam — and why not, poems are even shorter — then make sure that it isn't all you do for the prose section (there might not be a question that allows for the short story) and make sure you know it and understand it well in terms of its form.

But, of course, prose includes non-fiction as well as novels and short stories. "Non-fiction" is a term which covers a great many kinds of books: travel books, biographies, autobiographies, essays and journalism. We read non-fiction *because* we want to learn something, whereas with fiction what we learn is almost by-the-way. When you study non-fiction then you must begin from that standpoint: what is it I have learned from this book or this essay or this piece of journalism?

All of us, as we grow up, develop what are called "received ideas" — attitudes and ways of thinking that we absorb quite uncritically from our parents, friends, immediate social environment, the press, television. Often our political outlook isn't something we have thought out for ourselves but is an expression of a whole set of beliefs we have somehow accepted without ever having thought about them, far less having challenged them. But it is not just in the area of politics — though by "politics" I mean really our beliefs about what human nature is like — that we have "received ideas": we have received ideas about authority, work, people of other races, people of other religions, foreigners, minority groups, women, men, marriage, friendship . . . the list is endless. The essay and some journalistic pieces can sometimes be the first real challenge we come across to our received notions. Non-fiction is usually written to convey and explore ideas, and in so doing enables us, the readers, to examine our own ideas and to see the flaws, weaknesses and, often, prejudices that run through them. We see our ideas in a fresh light; we can begin to challenge our ways of looking at things with an intellectual vigour that is as rewarding as it is illuminating.

Your study of non-fiction, then, has to be open-minded. Concentrate not just on what you have learned from the piece, but on how you have been challenged, how your ideas have altered as a result of having read it.

The next stage is to examine carefully how — the ways in which — the author presents his argument. The role of narrative (and by "narrative" I mean "the story") is less important in non-fiction, but is nevertheless still present. In *Shooting an Elephant* by George Orwell, for example, the narrative is really quite an important element in conveying what it is he wants to say. The essay is about (among other things) the nature of authority and how the authority figure is not free to be authoritarian but has to act in a way in which those over whom he has "power" expect him to act. To make this point he tells the story of the time he had to shoot an elephant. The narrative is the vehicle that carries the theme. (Narrative should not be confused with plot: *narrative* is the re-telling of events in their time-sequence, whereas *plot* is the deliberate construction of events with some notion of explanation or cause. The traditional example will serve: "The King died and then the Queen died" is narrative, whereas "The King died and then the Queen died of grief" is plot.)

You should also concentrate on the language features of the piece of non-fiction you are studying as well as the structure. Look carefully at the following extract from *Shooting an Elephant* where Orwell describes the death of the elephant, *and remember all that has been said about Practical Criticism.*

> The crowd grew very still, and a deep, low, happy sigh, as of people who see the theatre curtain go up at last, breathed from innumerable throats. They were going to have their bit of fun after all. The rifle was a beautiful German thing with cross-hair sights. I did not then know that in shooting an elephant one would shoot to cut an imaginary bar running from ear-hole to ear-hole. I ought, therefore, as the elephant was sideways on, to have aimed straight at his ear-hole; actually I aimed several inches in front of this, thinking the brain would be further forward.
> When I pulled the trigger I did not hear the bang or feel the

kick — one never does when a shot goes home — but I heard the devilish roar of glee that went up from the crowd. In that instant, in too short a time, one would have thought, even for the bullet to get there, a mysterious, terrible change had come over the elephant. He neither stirred nor fell, but every line of his body had altered. He looked suddenly stricken, shrunken, immensely old, as though the frightful impact of the bullet had paralysed him without knocking him down. At last, after what seemed a long time — it might have been five seconds, I dare say — he sagged flabbily to his knees. His mouth slobbered. An enormous senility seemed to have settled upon him. One could have imagined him thousands of years old. I fired again into the same spot. At the second shot he did not collapse but climbed with desperate slowness to his feet and stood weakly upright, with legs sagging and head drooping. I fired a third time. That was the shot that did for him. You could see the agony of it jolt his whole body and knock the last remnant of strength from his legs. But in falling he seemed for a moment to rise, for as his hind legs collapsed beneath him he seemed to tower upwards like a huge rock toppling, his trunk reaching skywards like a tree. He trumpeted, for the first and only time. And then down he came, his belly towards me, with a crash that seemed to shake the ground even where I lay.

I got up. The Burmans were already racing past me across the mud. It was obvious that the elephant would never rise again, but he was not dead. He was breathing very rhythmically with long rattling gasps, his great mound of side painfully rising and falling. His mouth was wide open — I could see far down into caverns of pale pink throat. I waited a long time for him to die, but his breathing did not weaken. Finally I fired my two remaining shots into the spot where I thought his heart must be. The thick blood welled out of him like red velvet, but still he did not die. His body did not even jerk when the shots hit him, the tortured breathing continued without a pause. He was dying, very slowly and in great agony, but in some world remote from me where not even a bullet could damage him further. I felt that I had got to put an end to that dreadful noise. It seemed dreadful to see the great beast lying there, powerless to move and yet powerless to die, and not even to be able to finish him. I sent back for my small rifle and poured shot after shot into his heart and down his throat.

They seemed to make no impression. The tortured gasps continued as steadily as the ticking of a clock.

In the end I could not stand it any longer and went away. I heard later that it took him half an hour to die. Burmans were bringing dahs and baskets even before I left, and I was told they had stripped his body almost to the bones by the afternoon.

From *Shooting an Elephant* by George Orwell.

What comes across most clearly is the genuineness of the writing. You know instinctively that it is based on experience. The parenthesis "— one never does when a shot goes home —" reinforces the realism. But what is remarkable is the absence of cliché. The writing is fresh and vivid: "a mysterious, terrible change had come over the elephant", "He looked suddenly stricken, shrunken, immensely old", "he sagged flabbily to his knees", "caverns of pale pink throat" and so on. Orwell is the master of direct, economical language: "That was the shot that did for him.", "I got up." — simple, short, but effective sentences. Some of his images are very unusual: his breathing was in "long rattling gasps". Look how effective "rattling" is (a word we would normally associate with wood vibrating) when associated with gasps. The gasps are also described as continuing "as steadily as the ticking of a clock". I could go on.

This piece of description is not essential to the theme he is conveying, but as a piece of reportage it is as accurate as it is vivid; it makes the reader feel as though he/she is there as an eye-witness too.

Finally I want to mention rhythm, a word normally associated with poetry. But prose has rhythm too, and Orwell is an author who can exploit rhythm for its dramatic effect. Look at the ending of *Shooting an Elephant*.

The older men said I was right, the younger men said it was a damn shame to shoot an elephant for killing a coolie, because an elephant was worth more than any damn Coringhee coolie. And afterwards I was very glad that the coolie had been killed; it put me legally in the right and it gave me sufficient pretext for shooting the elephant. I often wondered whether any of the others grasped that I had done it solely to avoid looking a fool.

Look at the first sentence: the parallel structure of "the older men said . . ., the younger men said . . ."; the repetition of coolie and elephant; the repetition of "damn" but its shift from describing "shame" to "coolie". The rhythm of the sentence captures the language, utterances and attitudes of the two generations. But what I admire is the dramatic effect of the final sentence; the climax is "to avoid looking a fool" but examine how he delays the climax by putting it right at the end of the sentence, and even the insertion of "solely" helps delay it further.

I have used *Shooting an Elephant* as an example. The technique, however, applies to any prose work you are studying.

Finally, I want to look closely at the beginning of *The Power and the Glory*, partly because it's important to be able to read a text closely, partly because it's important to examine how an author establishes theme and atmosphere and partly because the kind of analysis we will undertake is the kind of analysis you will be expected to perform in the Specified Texts section. It has to be stressed, however, that *The Power and the Glory* is **not** a set text at the moment. Of course, this is also an exercise in practical criticism — do you see how in English all the skills come together? A development of your skills in answering one bit of the paper will help develop your skills in another. It's really quite simple!

Extract from

The Power and the Glory

CHAPTER I

The Port

MR TENCH went out to look for his ether cylinder, into the blazing Mexican sun and the bleaching dust. A few vultures looked down from the roof with shabby indifference: he wasn't carrion yet. A faint feeling of rebellion stirred in Mr Tench's heart, and he wrenched up a piece of the road with splintering finger-nails and tossed it feebly towards them. One rose and flapped across the town: over the tiny plaza over the bust of an ex-president, ex-general, ex-human being, over the two stalls which sold mineral water, towards the river and the sea. It wouldn't find anything there: the sharks looked after the carrion on that side. Mr Tench went on across the plaza.

He said 'Buenos días' to a man with a gun who sat in a small patch of shade against a wall. But it wasn't like England: the man said nothing at all, just stared malevolently up at Mr Tench, as if he had never had any dealings with the foreigner, as if Mr Tench were not responsible for his two gold bicuspid teeth. Mr Tench went sweating by, past the Treasury which once had been a church, towards the quay. Half-way across he suddenly forgot what he had come out for — a glass of mineral water? That was all there was to drink in this prohibition state — except beer, but that was a government monopoly and too expensive except on special occasions. An awful feeling of nausea gripped Mr Tench in the stomach — it couldn't have been mineral water he wanted. Of course his ether cylinder . . . the boat was in. He had heard its exultant piping while he lay on his bed after lunch. He passed the barbers' and two dentists and came out between a warehouse and the customs on to the river bank.

From *The Power and the Glory* by Graham Greene

Every line, every word of this novel is chosen with deliberate care for the right effect. The very first two words of the novel are "Mr Tench": ask yourself about the sound of the word "Tench" — what does it sound like? Remind you of? Stench? Tension? What other word does it suggest? Tench — the fish. But look carefully at the whole of the sentence. Mr Tench goes out to look for his ether cylinder and all that it suggests about anaesthetising feelings and pain. And when he goes out, it is into the "blazing sun" and "bleaching dust" — the sun, normally associated with life and life-giving forces, is here associated with Hell ("blazing") and death ("bleaching dust"). "Bleaching dust" also conjures up the picture of bones lying whitened by the sun slowly becoming ashes: "ashes to ashes, dust to dust". You'll note we move from "bleaching dust" to "vultures" — ugly scavengers which live off death; the vultures look with "shabby indifference" but ignore Tench because he isn't yet "carrion". He throws a piece of the road at them and one flaps across the town. The reader follows its flight over the "bust of an ex-president, ex-general, ex-human being" (note the list in climactic structure, the repetition of "ex", the irony of "human being"), over the two stalls which sold mineral water (no alcohol in this puritanical state), out over the river towards the sea. The river and the sea represent escape from this fascist state, but we find the sea is full of sharks which "look after the carrion on that side" — in other words there is no escape. The gun is a symbol which runs through this novel, a symbol to which we are introduced in paragraph two. Mr Tench says "'Buenos días' to a man with a gun" as he walks across the plaza, past "the Treasury which had once been a church" and here we have echoes of the temple which had been taken over by the moneylenders whom Christ eventually expelled.

Right at the beginning of the novel is established the run-down stultifying, death-ridden nature of the Mexican State from which there is no escape, except through death itself. In other words a writer with this kind of skill can establish both atmosphere and one of the major themes of his novel in two short paragraphs.

The Specified Text question will ask questions which will demand the kinds of response outlined above. You need to know about the passage set, but also about the immediate context and its relationship to the novel as a whole. Look carefully, though, at the number of marks awarded since they will be a guide to the amount you are required to write.

– 7 –

POETRY

Poetry is perhaps the genre most feared and hated by candidates and yet it is often the genre best handled (in the actual examination), especially and ironically by boys. The great advantage, for an unwilling schoolfellow, that poetry has over drama and prose, is that poems are usually short. You may spend in preparation for the exam six weeks or longer (in class), studying *Hamlet*, yet only 30 minutes on a poem: both in the exam itself are worth the same in terms of marks. You might find *The Practical Guide to Poetry* by David Cockburn (Robert Gibson & Sons) an added help.

The problem for most students is how to go about studying poetry, or even how to go about reacting to it. Nothing is more guaranteed to bring about embarrassed blushes and stammers than to ask a pupil what he thinks of a poem we have just read in class. The problem often is not knowing where to begin. But you must remember that unlike other genres of literature, poetry is very "dense", it's very complex. You have to read a poem several times, and with a lot of skill, to reveal all its meanings. Reading a poem can be a bit like peeling an onion: each layer of meaning is stripped off at each reading. It's only to be hoped the peeling of the poem won't cause so many tears!

All that you have read so far will help you cope with the reading of a poem. Always go back to the three questions set out earlier in this book.

(a)   What is the poem about?

(b)   What effects does it have on me?

(c)   How are these effects achieved?

Read carefully the following poem by Ted Hughes:

The Jaguar

The apes yawn and adore their fleas in the sun.
The parrots shriek as if they were on fire, or strut
Like cheap tarts to attract the stroller with the nut,
Fatigued with indolence, tiger and lion.

Lie still as the sun. The boa-constrictor's coil
Is a fossil. Cage after cage seems empty, or
Stinks of sleepers from the breathing straw.
It might be painted on a nursery wall.

But who runs like the rest past these arrives
At a cage where the crowd stands, stares, mesmerised,
As a child at a dream, at a jaguar hurrying enraged
Through prison darkness after the drills of his eyes

On a short fierce fuse. Not in boredom —
The eye satisfied to be blind in fire,
By the bang of blood in the brain deaf the ear —
He spins from the bars, but there's no cage to him

More than to the visionary his cell:
His stride is wildernesses of freedom:
The world rolls under the long thrust of his heel.
Over the cage floor the horizons come.

From *The Hawk in the Rain* by Ted Hughes.

You must read the poem several times and as you read it listen to the sound of the poem.

Ask yourself what you think the poem is about. You will probably come up with more than one answer: the boredom animals suffer in captivity; the attraction the jaguar has for the crowds; the inability the jaguar has to accept the zoo; the power of the jaguar's imagination, and so on. But, next, look at the effects of the poem. Using a pencil, go through the poem and mark the language features:

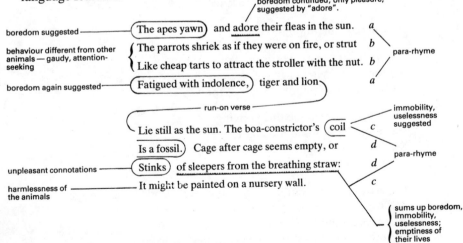

43

You should now go through the remainder of the poem doing the same thing: the more you read it the more you will find to make comments on. As you do this you build up simultaneously your knowledge of the poem and your notes for the exam. Hughes uses many striking phrases about the jaguar: "blind in fire", "bang of blood in the brain", "more than to the visionary his cell", "wildernesses of freedom", "the long thrust of his heel". What do each of these phrases suggest to you? Work on words such as "visionary" and "wilderness" — together they could refer to something religious. Look at the contrast between "cell" and "wildernesses".

Sometimes you will be puzzled and will struggle to make sense of what the poet has written, but don't worry about it. Poems are deliberately complex and difficult — usually because they represent a difficult and complex bit of experience. They cannot be summed up, summarised or translated; but far from stopping your enjoyment of them, their very complexity can add to it. That's why you will continue to discover levels of meaning in a poem years after your first encounter with it.

Let's look at another poem, this time by D.H. Lawrence.

Bat

At evening, sitting on this terrace,
When the sun from the west, beyond Pisa, beyond the
    mountains of Carrara
Departs, and the world is taken by surprise . . .

When the tired flower of Florence is in gloom beneath the
    glowing
Brown hills surrounding . . .

When under the arches of the Ponte Vecchio
A green light enters against stream, flush from the west,
Against the current of obscure Arno . . .

Look up, and you see things flying
Between the day and the night;
Swallows with spools of dark thread sewing the shadows
    together

A circle swoop, and a quick parabola under the bridge
    arches
Where light pushes through;
A sudden turning upon itself of a thing in the air.
A dip to the water.

And you think:
"The swallows are flying so late!"

Swallows?

Dark air-life looping
Yet missing the pure loop . . .
A twitch, a twitter, an elastic shudder in flight
And serrated wings against the sky,
Like a glove, a black glove thrown up at the light,
And falling back.

Never swallows!
Bats!
The swallows are gone.

At a wavering instant the swallows gave way to bats
By the Ponte Vecchio . . .
Changing guard.

Bats, and an uneasy creeping in one's scalp
As the bats swoop overhead!
Flying madly.

Pipistrello!
Black piper on an infinitesimal pipe.
Little lumps that fly in air and have voices indefinite, wildly
    vindictive;

Wings like bits of umbrella.

Bats!

Creatures that hang themselves up like an old rag, to sleep;
And disgustingly upside down.
Hanging upside down like rows of disgusting old rags
And grinning in their sleep.
Bats!

In China the bat is a symbol of happiness

Not for me!

From *Bat* by D.H. Lawrence.

You'll agree that this time it's easy to say what this poem is about. It is fairly self-explanatory: the poet is sitting in the evening by the Ponte Vecchio in Florence, Italy. He notices, almost absently, the swallows and then realises, with disgust, that the creatures are not swallows but bats. What is interesting is the way the poet creates the effects he does.

The poem is written in blank verse — there is no rhyme scheme — and it is in free verse — there is no regular rhythm. The verses are more like paragraphs, and are, in fact, referred to as verse paragraphs. Note how, in the first three verse paragraphs, he creates the feeling of relaxation — the evening, sitting on a terrace, sunset — and the feeling of lethargy — "tired flower of Florence". Each verse is a kind of snapshot or, more accurately, a kind of unfinished painting, the three dots indicating that the reader's imagination has to supply what is missing. Florence was the centre of renaissance art, but is no longer, hence the "tired flower of Florence" — it has passed its best.

He notes the swallows, but it is almost absent-mindedly — "things flying / Between the day and the night". It is not an unpleasant image — "spools of dark thread" which sew the shadows together, a "circle swoop", the "sudden turning upon itself of a thing in the air".

The poet pays a little more attention and muses that the swallows are flying late. The doubt: "Swallows?". He begins to notice the detail and the words become unpleasant: "missing the pure loop" — echoing, negatively, "spool" and "loop". Then really unpleasant words such as "twitch", "twitter", "elastic shudder", "serrated", "a black glove thrown up at the night". The full realisation of truth comes with the single monosyllabic "Bats!" with the hard "b", almost like a swear word. The truth brings with it the "uneasy creeping" in his scalp, and his images create feelings of disgust and repulsion: "Little lumps that fly in air", "voices indefinite, wildly vindictive", "Wings like bits of umbrella". The latter image is particularly appropriate because of its visual accuracy, especially when he says the wings are like "bits" of umbrella. He uses repetition effectively — in the next line "Bats" repeats (nearly) "bits". I like the cleverness of the next four lines:

> Creatures that hang themselves up like an old rag, to sleep;
> And disgustingly upside down.
> Hanging upside down like rows of disgusting old rags
> And grinning in their sleep.

The repetition of "upside down" in the next line almost creates the impression of *being* upside down, but what is really clever is how he changes the repeated word enough to avoid boredom — "hang" becomes "hanging", and "disgustingly" changes to "disgusting".

Lawrence chooses words very carefully for their connotative area. Why, for example, does he choose "grinning" rather than "smiling"?

Bat is a simple poem which is technically clever and poetically effective: it captures a bit of experience — a detestation of bats — and re-creates the feelings we have for them. It is a very accurate poem.

You can see that we never lose sight of the three questions:

(a) What is the poem about?

(b) What are the effects that it has on me?

(c) How have these effects been achieved?

In many ways, of course, by far the most difficult of these questions is the last one:

How have these effects been achieved?

That is the questions that is at the basis of the practical criticism technique. Of course you need to be sensitive enough to know what the effect is on you (though even the totally insensitive are aware of being bored!), but, for the purposes of preparing for this Higher, and, really, in order to become a critical and intelligent reader, you need to know **how** the author got whatever effect you felt.

Let's try it again, this time with *Lady Lazarus* by Sylvia Plath. Immediate question: who was *Lazarus*? And therefore who might *Lady Lazarus* be? Keep the three questions in mind, but we really do want to concentrate on that last question.

Lady Lazarus

I have done it again.
One year in every ten
I manage it —

A sort of walking miracle, my skin
Bright as a Nazi lampshade,
My right foot

A paperweight,
My face a featureless, fine
Jew linen.

Peel off the napkin
O my enemy.
Do I terrify?

The nose, the eye pits, the full set of teeth?
The sour breath
Will vanish in a day.

Soon, soon the flesh
The grave cave ate will be
At home on me

And I a smiling woman.
I am only thirty.
And like the cat I have nine times to die.

This is Number Three.
What a trash
To annihilate each decade.

What a million filaments.
The peanut-crunching crowd
Shoves in to see

Them unwrap me hand and foot —
The big strip tease.
Gentlemen, ladies

These are my hands
My knees.
I may be skin and bone,

Nevertheless, I am the same, identical woman.
The first time it happened I was ten.
It was an accident.

The second time I meant
To last it out and not come back at all.
I rocked shut

As a seashell.
They had to call and call
And pick the worms off me like sticky pearls.

Dying
Is an art, like everything else.
I do it exceptionally well.

I do it so it feels like hell.
I do it so it feels real.
I guess you could say I've a call.

It's easy enough to do it in a cell.
It's easy enough to do it and stay put.
It's the theatrical

Comeback in broad day
To the same place, the same face, the same brute
Amused shout:

'A miracle!'
That knocks me out.
There is a charge

For the eyeing of my scars, there is a charge
For the hearing of my heart —
It really goes.

And there is a charge, a very large charge
For a word or a touch
Or a bit of blood

Or a piece of my hair or my clothes.
So, so, Herr Doktor.
So, Herr Enemy.

I am your opus,
I am your valuable,
The pure gold baby

That melts to a shriek.
I turn and burn.
Do not think I underestimate your great concern.

Ash, ash —
You poke and stir.
Flesh, bone, there is nothing there —

A cake of soap,
A wedding ring,
A gold filling.

Herr God, Herr Lucifer
Beware
Beware.

Out of the ash
I rise with my red hair
And I eat men like air.

From Lady Lazarus by Sylvia Plath.

Have you found out why 'Lazarus'? You need to know about the story of Lazarus and how Christ raised him from the dead to be able to get the allusion. The title will then be a help to the understanding of the poem.

Establish first of all what the poem is about. Plath is talking about her attempts at committing suicide, and the poem concerns itself with the efforts of the medical profession to pull her round after "Number Three".

There are allusions — references — in this poem to The Nazis and to the entertainment industry, references which appear elsewhere in Plath's poetry. She talks of her skin being as "Bright as a Nazi lampshade", her foot being used "as a paperweight": both references to the atrocities Nazis performed on the Jews, where the skin of a Jew was used as a lampshade, and their feet were used as paperweights. She talks about "the big strip tease" (a reference to the removal of her bandages) which "The peanut crunching crowd / shoves in to see" (a reference to the public's casual, uncaring interest in her revival). But with what do we associate "strip tease" and "the peanut crunching crowd"? Yes, you are right, the entertainment industry. What, then, is she saying about what happens to Lady lazarus when she is revived? How does she feel if the removal of her bandages is like a "strip tease", and if the doctors and hospital staff are like "a peanut crunching crowd" who "shove in to see"? Americans chew peanuts at the cinema or at their version of shows or amusement parks: what does the fact that they are chewing peanuts and shoving their way in to look at her imply about their attitude to her?

But what is really interesting about this poem is in the authoress's use of language and poetic technique. Given all that I've said about structure, connotation, rhythm, rhyme, sound, repetition, go through the poem and comment fully on these devices.

Why, towards the end of the poem, does she refer to her docter as "Herr Doktor" and "Herr Enemy"? What is the image at the end of the poem? Is it appropriate? How does this poem relate to others by Sylvia Plath?

We are asking questions about effects and how they have been created, and as you jot down your answers to these questions in your notebook, you are recording your own notes. And much better they will be than any you can buy because your notes record what **you** think and not what someone else thinks. Your genuine reaction to and interest in the literature that you are studying is **exactly** what the examiners are looking for.

– 8 –

REVIEW OF PERSONAL STUDIES

The *Review of Personal Reading* has to be produced as part of the Folio and presented to the Scottish Examination Board in Dalkeith by 31st March of the year in which you sit your Higher English. According to the Revised Arrangements Document, your Review should be a work of **personal** investigation, between 1000 and 1500 words long, into a work of literature or Media Studies.

Revised Arrangements also says that:

(a) your Review should take the form of a detailed study of a single literary text or set of short texts or a comparison of two or more texts;

(b) you should choose your own text;

(c) your choice should be made from imaginative literature, biography, memoirs, essays or journalism;

(d) you may compare a literary text with its non-print version, e.g. you may compare a novel with its film adaptation;

(e) you **must not** use any text that is central to your RPR anywhere else in the examination.

This task sounds utterly daunting, but if you follow my advice then you should find it more straightforward than you at first imagine. One thing you **must** do is plan how you set about tackling your RPR: what you **must not** and **cannot** do is to leave everything to the last minute. And by last minute I mean the beginning of March. You really have to begin the work for your RPR as early as you possibly can.

You ask: *Where do I begin?* and *How should I begin?* Well, you really must begin by thinking about the kinds of books, plays, and poems that you have so far enjoyed studying in English. One of the main keys to success in the RPR is to be interested and involved in the text that is going to be the basis of your answer. In fact, when the marker comes to examine your RPR one of the things he/she will be told to look for is the extent to which you have demonstrated that interest. Now one thing that is difficult to fake, as no doubt you have learned to your cost in the classroom, is interest. Your interest really does have to be genuine. And the text really does have to be your own choice.

Choosing the Text

You must choose for yourself the text you want to work on. You may consult your teacher about that choice, but the important thing to remember is that your teacher is not allowed to choose the text for you. It is a review of **personal** reading.

Begin the job of choosing as early as you can: certainly have your choice made by the January of the year in which you are to sit the examination. You can of course, choose earlier than that, but in some schools teachers may want you to try a "dummy run" at the RPR, in which case you will have to make a choice for the dummy run maybe as early as the September of the year **before** you sit the examination. You should start by thinking of the kinds of texts that you enjoyed reading and studying in your Fourth Year. I shall guess, and there's a pretty good chance that I am right, that you will choose prose: a novel or some short stories. My advice to you is to think again. Since the vast majority of RPR's involve the novel, you would do well to think about poetry or drama. There are far too few RPR's which have poetry or drama as their basis, and you would do well to give some consideration to any poems you have recently grown to like or to a play that has caught your imagination. But please do not think about using texts that you have studied the year before. You must choose material that is fresh to you.

Another thing you must not do is base your RPR on some work of popular fiction such as *The Guns of Navarone*; not because I think that is an inferior novel, but because it is the kind of fiction that you will have difficulty in finding much to say about — and remember you have to find 1000 – 1500 words. If the text you have chosen is an easy read, then the chances are that it is not a very demanding text, and as such you will find that there is not a lot you can say about it. My advice, then, is that the more challenging the text, the more you will be able to write. And, ironically, the more interested you are likely to become in it.

OK, you ask, *what things should I bear in mind when I am choosing the text for my RPR?* Let me list them:

(a)   *The book, play, or poem (and please remember what I have said about choosing poetry and drama)* **must** *interest you — do not choose to write about a text that bores you because you will communicate that boredom to the examiner effectively and detrimentally.*

Higher English **demands** evidence of personal interest in and engagement with the texts you have chosen to write about, not just here, but in Paper II as well. You must demonstrate in your RPR that you like the text you have chosen and that it has said something of interest to **you,** If you don't, it is conceivable that you may not pass.

(b)   *The text you choose must be able to provide you with plenty to write about.*

You may enjoy a popular text that is easy to read, but it may not stimulate you into writing much. A more "difficult" text will offer you plenty on which you can comment.

(c)   *The text must have something to say to you as a person.*

The text you choose must have something to say to you personally. Maybe there is a character with whom you identify, a setting with which you are familiar, a situation you recognise, or a theme that means a lot to you. You must **personally** choose the text, and you must **personally** be involved in it.

Let us now assume that you have chosen the text and that it meets all three of the requirements above. What next? Well, you must become very familiar with the text: read it over and over again until your knowledge of it is thorough. Oh, and you must buy yourself a little notebook! Then you set yourself the famous three questions:

(a)   *What is* (let's assume you have chosen to do a poem — wisely) *the poem about?*

(b)   *What effects does it have on me?*

(c)   *How has the author achieved these effects?*

The answer to *(a)* above is very important when it comes to the RPR, because the answer to this question will provide you with the themes that the

54

poem has **for you**. Remember, don't answer this question in terms of plot: look again at what I said, or, rather, at what Dawn and Tracy said on page 10. One advantage of studying poetry for your RPR is that you will be less inclined to want to retell plot since, by and large, poems don't really have plots. Candidates who tackle novels (the majority — remember) find it almost impossible to tear themselves away from the plot! Answer our question, then, in terms of *themes*. For example, you might jot down in your notebook that your chosen poem is about *the evanescence of youth* or about how we *become victims of old age* or about *unrequited love* or about *jealousy*. You now have your theme, and the point is that it really is your theme: you are declaring your personal interest in the poem by saying what it is about for you.

Once you have stated the theme or themes, you have to go on and say how these themes are established and developed. Look at the very beginning of the poem. Where does the poet establish the theme you have chosen to write about? How does he go on to develop it? Does he add to it, qualify it, exemplify it? Note down all your answers.

Now, of course you are not expected to be the world's most sensitive and most perspicacious reader (if you are not sure about "perspicacious", look it up and jot down the meaning somewhere else in your notebook). Even someone as experienced and as clever as your teacher had to consult other people at sometime in his/her career when studying texts. You may have noticed yourself that, after having seen a film or a television play with a friend, as you begin to talk to each other about it, your ideas about the film or play change or become more definite or more developed. It is not forbidden to talk to your teacher about your poem, to chat over with him/her the ideas you have so far thought about. Nor is it forbidden to consult the better quality commercially-produced notes. What is unwise is to depend on your teacher or those notes for your ideas, and what is absolutely forbidden is for you to copy down what your teacher has said or to copy out the notes you have bought. The ideas have to be your own, but there is no harm in talking them over with an expert or consulting what an expert has written. This whole process should be about building up your relationship with your chosen poem and not depending on someone else's.

Next, we have to think about author technique: in other words we have to answer the third question — how does the author achieve the effects?

Perhaps the most interesting area when it comes to the study of literature is the area of author technique. Let's start with yourself. Since you were at primary school, you have been asked to write essays and to create short stories; in other words, for about ten or twelve years now you have been striving to be an accomplished author. So, how do you go about your writing? Let us be even more specific: you have been set a task by your teacher to write about the theme of jealousy and how it can affect friendship, and you have been told that you can choose to write either discursively or creatively. How do you begin? Clearly, you have to begin by making choices. And the first choice has to be: *Am I going to write a discursive essay on the nature of jealousy within friendship or is it going to be a short story with such a topic as its theme?* Let us assume that you have chosen to write a short story. What next? Again you are faced with choices — choices to do with where you are going to set the story, when you are going to set it, who are the main characters, and, possibly most importantly, what is going to happen. The point I am really trying to make is that stories, novels, plays, poems, whatever, don't just *occur*: someone, quite deliberately, puts them together in a certain order and in a certain way. You do that when you write, as do all authors. We as readers, as critical readers, can study just **how** these stories, novels, plays and poems have been put together. In so doing, we are studying *author technique* and that is precisely what you have to do next for your RPR — study author technique. By now you will have realised that we are answering the third question:

(c) How has the author achieved these effects?

This question is to do with Practical Criticism: the examination of the ways in which the author has created the effects that he has had on you. If you have chosen to study a poem for your RPR, then by now you have made your notes on the themes suggested by the poem, the effects created by the poet, and the ways in which he created those effects. And you have got these notes by answering the three questions set above.

Once all that preparation has been done the next thing you must do is set yourself a task. Again, your teacher is not allowed to set the task for you, but of course he/she is allowed to give you advice about the task you want to tackle. It may be that in his/her opinion the task you have chosen is too easy or too difficult or else your teacher may feel that it won't allow you to demonstrate all the skills that you have acquired. The task, however, must interest you; it must be such that it will get you engaged in the writing process and allow you to demonstrate that engagement as you write.

Actually, if you have done your note-taking thoroughly and conscientiously, then the task should suggest itself. You should have an idea of what it is you want to say about the text you have studied.

Let us now suppose that you have done all the preparation, you have selected your task, and you are well into the writing of your RPR. The next thing that you will want to know is if you are on the right lines. What is it, you may well be asking, that the examiners are looking for? Fortunately, the question is easy to answer. To begin with, you should put that question to your teacher because your school will have in its possession a document from the Scottish Examination Board explaining in great detail how the RPR is marked. I can put it very simply for you. The examiners are really looking for four things:

(a) *Your knowledge of the text.* You must show in your RPR that you have read the text and are familiar with it.

(b) *Your understanding of the ideas in the text.* You must show to the examiners that you understand the ideas raised by the text and have a grasp of its themes.

(c) *Your understanding of the author's techniques.* You must make it clear that you are familiar with the various techniques deployed by the author — what we talked about above. Don't just quote a bit and then say 'isn't that a lovely metaphor' or 'what an exciting bit of onomatopoeia'. Say instead what is appropriate about the metaphor or how he has achieved the onomatopoeia.

(d) *Your genuine personal interest.* This is what I have been stressing all along. In order to achieve half marks in the RPR you must demonstrate that you have been involved in the text and have got something out of it. The examiners are told to look for this quality and they are further told that if it is not present then it is unlikely that the RPR will pass.

Finally, you should remember that the stipulated word length is between 1000 and 1500 words. Don't sell yourself short by producing a mere 800 words, but on the other hand please limit your RPR to a maximum of 1500 words. Too many RPRs reach astronomical limits and penalise themselves in the process. If your RPR is too long, look again at the first page because if there is anywhere that you can wield a blue pencil, I am willing to wager that it's there. Too often in the first page, candidates waste words recounting plot: if you have done that, get rid of it. It is comment that matters not a rehash of the text.

Since, however, this chapter is not about how to write your RPR, I shan't go into any more detail in that area; the book, after all, is about literature and literary technique, not about writing. If you are concerned about how to set about writing your RPR then you should consult *The Practical Guide to Revised Higher English* by David Cockburn (Robert Gibson & Sons).

But do bear in mind all that has been said in this chapter, and please do not read it in isolation from the rest. You need to know a great deal about how to study literature and that topic is a matter for more than this chapter alone.

– 9 –

THE EXAMINATION ITSELF

Paper II — The Specified Texts

One thing you must do before the examination — if you are contemplating this section of the paper, especially if you are attempting this Higher on your own — is to check with a teacher, a tutor, or alternatively with the Scottish Examination Board, as to which Specified Texts are being set in any given year. The Board is committed to changing some of the texts every three years; the last thing you want is to have prepared, with the thoroughness that this section requires, a text which has just dropped out of the examination! There is little point in my reproducing the current list of Specified Texts here since within a year the list would be out-of-date and therefore not just misleading but downright mischievous. Check the current list. If you are in any doubt, contact the Scottish Education Board in Ironmills Road, Dalkeith, Midlothian; they will be only too delighted to supply you with the necessary information.

I can actually offer you a crumb of comfort for this paper. If you have read all of this book thus far very carefully and have done all the things I have suggested; if you have prepared for the writing of your RPR in the way that I have suggested; if, indeed, you have written your RPR in the way in which I have indicated, then you will be well able to reach all the parts of Paper II — successfully. Preparation is all. One advantage to the structure of this paper is that you can look at the Specified Texts section, the Practical Criticism section, the Drama section, the Poetry section, the Prose section and the Media Studies section, all together, and then make up your mind as to how you will plot your way through the paper.

With Specified Texts you can expect three kinds of questions:

(a) *questions about the immediate context;*

(b) *questions on and about the passage itself;*

(c) *questions demanding knowledge and understanding of other parts of the text or of other poems.*

But always, however many questions there are and whatever they are like, look very carefully at the number of marks available since that will indicate the length of answer being demanded. A question, for example, which asks you for two marks to comment on some aspect of language in the passage isn't asking for much in the way of detail.

Paper II — Practical Criticism

In many ways this book has been all about Practical Criticism. It is the most important skill to develop if you want to become a critical and intelligent reader of books, poetry, journals and newspapers. I also very firmly believe that the only way to teach literature and the only way to study it is through the continual development of practical criticism skills. Otherwise you merely reiterate what someone else thinks about the text in question, and that can be satisfactory for no-one. You must make up your own mind about the texts you have chosen to study. But you aren't out there entirely on your own — there is a framework which will help you form your ideas: the three questions.

(a) *What is the text about? [Answer in themes.]*

(b) *What effects does it have on me? [Answer in terms of your reactions — laugh, cry, felt sad, etcetera.]*

(c) *How has the author created these effects? [Answer in terms of techniques.]*

What I am really saying is that if you have prepared for this examination in the way in which I have recommended then you are well prepared for the Practical Criticism section and you must therefore think of it as a serious option on the day of the exam. If anyone tells you to forget the PC, remember this: the Interpretation in Paper I will have several PC-type questions, therefore you cannot escape PC no matter how much it is suggested you try. Moreover, since many of the questions in the Specified Text will also be PC-type questions, there is no escape for anyone there either. Don't ignore Practical Criticism.

Paper II — The Critical Essay

What far too many candidates do in their preparation for this paper is to buy a set of commercially produced notes, digest them in their entirety, and regurgitate them on the day of the examination no matter what the question asked. If you have studied your chosen texts in the way in which I have recommended then you have no need to purchase anyone else's ideas because you will have plenty of your own. Make your own notes from the very beginning. Decide for yourself what the themes of your chosen texts are, what issues they deal with. Then decide how these themes get established, how they are developed, what role the characters play, what significance the setting has, etcetera. In other words, as you answer *(a)*, *(b)* and *(c)* on page 60, write down your responses — they will form the basis of your own notes, which will have the merit of being your own and therefore highly personal — a demand of this examination.

There are three main reasons for most of the failures in this part of the examination and they are all related to the over-use of commercially produced notes:

(i) not answering the question asked;

(ii) not giving a personal response;

(iii) not producing a sufficiently adequate answer.

If you have spent money, time and effort mugging up what somebody terribly important has had to say about *Macbeth* or *Death of a Salesman*, then the temptation to write all that you have learned down in the examination is almost impossible to overcome. Yet, all those hard-conned notes, pitchforked into your answer because you spent hours learning them — besides you have nothing else to say — far from helping you in your time of need are, in fact, the cause of your downfall. Examiners are experts at detecting notes — the ideas themselves and the way that they are expressed are so obviously not the candidate's. Notes, almost by definition, prevent you from expressing your opinion about the book, and, as I have told you repeatedly, there are many marks available for expressing a personal response. And if you are dependent on notes, you will run out of ideas in your answer, producing a short, inadequate response that is derivative and devoid of personal involvement.

What should I do then? Look carefully at the question, break it down into its parts, select from your own knowledge of the text what is relevant in answering the demands of the question, and ensure that you communicate to the examiner some enthusiasm for the text in question. The secret lies in being well prepared, of course, but also in planning your answer before you start to write it. The readiness is all.

– 10 –

CONCLUSION

Literature, if we know how to read it, can tell us something about ourselves, about life, about the nature of existence itself. Reading *Hamlet* isn't quite the same thing as reading the side of an HP Sauce bottle: *Hamlet* is more demanding — it requires a higher level reading skill. The main purpose of this book is to help you develop as much reading skill as you can, though a book can only begin the process. The rest is up to you. You must practise reading the way that you practise any other skill if you want to keep it in shape.

This book has also been about preparing your literature studies for the Higher English Examination, though I hasten to add that the sole purpose of literature is not so that seventeen year-olds will beat out their brains in some desperate examination hall or so that some poor marker can find, in an even more desperate study, solace in the fact that he knows the *exact* words that Macbeth said and has a red pen to prove it.

Literature isn't some geometric theorem to be conned by rote and recited at will. But the examination has to be prepared for, like it or not, and this book aims to make that preparation easier and a little more palatable. The only method is by the close study of your chosen text. Think out for yourself what the themes or issues are for you, and then work out what scenes, characters, images establish, illustrate and develop those themes. Such a close study of the text will, at the same time, develop your skills at Practical Criticism, and as you develop your skills in Practical Criticism you will learn to read with greater sensitivity, understanding and awareness. Nothing is in compartments in English; each skill affects the development of the other.

In your answers, choose the questions that best suit the texts that you have studied, be relevant, answer exactly what is asked, write formally, be genuine, and, above all, refer very closely to the text itself to demonstrate to the examiner your knowledge and your understanding. Never make a point about a book without backing it up with evidence from the text. And remember, literature is there to challenge our ideas, to help us develop as human beings, to enrich our lives, and, above all, to be enjoyed. Remember that, and tell the examiner about it in the month of May.

ACKNOWLEDGEMENTS

The author and publishers are grateful to the following for permission to use copyright material in this book.

Under Milk Wood
by Dylan Thomas.
Reprinted by permission of the Publisher J.M. Dent & Sons, Ltd.

The Castle
From *The Collected Poems* of Edwin Muir.
Reprinted by permission of the Publisher Faber & Faber Ltd.

Shooting an Elephant
From *Selected Writings* by George Orwell.
Reprinted by permission of the Publisher Octopus Books Ltd

The Power and the Glory
by Graham Greene.
Reprinted by permission of the author's agents Laurence Pollinger Ltd., and the Publishers William Heinemann Ltd. and The Bodley Head Ltd.

The Jaguar
From *The Hawk in the Rain*
by Ted Hughes.
Reprinted by permission of the Publisher Faber & Faber Ltd.

Bat
by D.H. Lawrence.
Reprinted by permission of the author's agents Laurence Pollinger Ltd. and the Estate of Mrs. Frieda Lawrence Ravagli.

Lady Lazarus
by Slyvia Plath.

The Publishers have made every effort to trace the ownership of copyright material and to secure permission from holders of such material. They regret any inadvertent error and will be pleased to make the necessary corrections in future printings.

Printed in Great Britain by
Martin's of Berwick Ltd.